Successful
Purchasing

Stephen Carter

BARRON'S

All inquiries should be addressed to:
Barron's Educational Series, Inc.
250 Wireless Boulevard
Hauppauge, New York 11788

Library of Congress Catalog Card Number 96-43002

International Standard Book No. 0-7641-0057-2

Library of Congress Cataloging-in-Publication Data
Carter, Stephen, 1944–
     Successful purchasing / Stephen Carter.
         p.   cm. — (Business success series)
     ISBN 0-7641-0057-2
     1. Purchasing. 2. Success in business. I. Title. II. Series.
HF5437.C372   1997
658.7'2—dc20   96-43002
                                                          CIP

PRINTED IN HONG KONG
987654321

Contents

Introduction

The nature of purchasing and supply is changing fast as more and more people begin to recognize the enormous impact it can have on a company's ability to prosper in today's fiercely competitive markets.

This means that the skills, personal characteristics, and objectives of a modern buyer are radically different from those of even a few years ago.

This book provides an easy-to-understand summary of the requirements of modern purchasing for buyers and all those involved in the buying process.

We will explore the following different aspects of these requirements.

The steps to understanding purchasing:

- *Role and scope*
- *Objectives and strategy*
- *Deciding what to buy*
- *Selecting and managing suppliers*
- *Determining the price*
- *Special purchases*
- *Performance measures*

Chapter 1

Role and Scope
of Purchasing

Although most people will readily admit that they neither like nor are good at selling, everyone believes he or she is a good buyer. We all buy things in our everyday lives and have honed our skills over the years. These skills are easily transferred to business life—or so we think!

In this section, we look at the role and scope of purchasing and how and why they have changed over the last few years. In particular, we will see why purchasing is increasingly becoming a battleground for competitive advantage as we approach the 21st century, and why the skills and strategies of buyers should not be taken for granted.

Although much of this section has a manufacturing perspective, the concepts are equally applicable to service and public organizations. We will look at the development of purchasing by considering:

◆ changes in business affecting purchasing.

◆ new pressures on purchasing.

◆ the tasks of a buyer.

◆ the role of suppliers.

◆ the role of buyers.

CHANGES IN BUSINESS AFFECTING PURCHASING

Business over the last three decades has seen several major initiatives, the end result being a fundamental change in the way purchasing operates.

The first was in the 1960s and 1970s when the marketing revolution took place. A company's product or service was tailored to meet the specific needs of individual market segments.

This resulted in much wider product ranges, ever shorter product life cycles, and increasingly higher quality standards as consumers became more discerning. In turn, this meant that buyers had to find suppliers who could develop a wider range of materials and parts, shorten their development timescales, and meet very stringent quality standards.

It was difficult to meet these customer needs and still make a profit using the traditional methods of manufacturing developed for mass-market products. This led to a second wave of initiatives in the 1980s that centered on manufacturing. These included Just-in-Time (JIT) manufacturing and total quality management (TQM), both of which address the people, process, and product-development issues that are directly under management's control.

However, although JIT and TQM go a long way towards aligning manufacturing operations with marketing strategy, their ultimate effectiveness is severely limited by the capability of suppliers to deliver defect-free materials and components in smaller, more frequent quantities at an affordable price.

A third change in business that affects purchasing is the way organizations are restructuring into sales units focused on customer requirements, with clear management responsibility and accountability.

This poses the question of where in the organization purchasing should be placed. One argument is that buyers should be situated in the sales units, as this makes them part of the team responsible for meeting the needs of a particular group of customers. They are then in a better position to meet customer requirements such as flexibility and responsiveness.

An alternative argument is that buyers should be in a centralized department where they can see the global needs of the organization and consolidate purchases to achieve lower costs. A centralized department can also afford specialized skills that individual sales units may not.

Whether centralized, decentralized, or a mixture of the two, purchasing has become less independent, taking on a service role to its internal customers in the sales units.

NEW PRESSURES ON PURCHASING

In addition to these changes, other pressures have emerged over the last few years. They include:

◆ a move to "get back to basics" in many companies, contracting out any operations that are not considered core activities. This increases the range, value, and complexity of the products and services they now purchase.

◆ the recognition that most of a new product's cost is decided at the design stage and so early supplier involvement can contribute greatly to lower costs. This has implications for the way that suppliers are selected and managed.

◆ pressure from environmental lobbyists putting the accent on reuse, preservation, and recycling. This means that suppliers must develop existing products or buyers must search for new ones.

◆ the recognition that more than half of the cost of quality in the manufacturing process is caused by the quality of items purchased from suppliers.

THE TASKS OF A BUYER

Faced with this array of changes and pressures, what should be the tasks of a modern buyer?

Open most textbooks on purchasing and they will probably tell you that the task of a buyer is to obtain the right goods, at the right price, at the right time, in the right quantity, and of the right quality. In other words, the traditional task of buyers centers on:

◆ ensuring short-term supply.

◆ improving cost competitiveness.

◆ ensuring long-term supply.

◆ contributing to product innovation.

Short-term availability is often the number one priority in the buying department, as failure in this area is very obvious to everyone, and can have severe financial repercussions if production is stopped as a result.

Once availability is assured, price reductions become the next priority. Buyers have long recognized that purchased components and raw materials account for anywhere between 50 percent and 80 percent of manufacturing costs. Add to this expenditure on services and capital items, and the scope for improving profits by reducing purchase prices is plain to see.

To achieve both these objectives, buyers often adopt confrontational approaches to supplier management that emphasize:

◆ bulk buying to get volume discounts and to keep unit costs down.

◆ high stock levels to maintain availability and compensate for inadequate quality.

◆ a large supplier base to create competitive pressure and provide alternatives for short-term supply.

◆ no long-term commitments.

◆ investment in order-processing and expediting systems to cope with the large number of purchase orders needed.

Unfortunately, this can lead to:

◆ long lead times.

◆ variable standards in supply and quality.

◆ no supplier involvement in new product development, product or process improvement, or cost reductions.

◆ high support costs.

◆ little trust and cooperation.

The result is the opposite of what the purchasing department needs from its supplier base.

THE ROLE OF SUPPLIERS

It is clear that a company needs the cooperation of its suppliers, particularly if it operates in fiercely competitive markets, where there is constant change and improvement in technology capability and customer expectations. The approaches to supplier management described previously do not encourage suppliers to enter into new ways of doing business.

For the key purchased items, the best way is to introduce the concept of partnership sourcing. This means both the buying and the supplying organizations form a close, long-term relationship and work together to gain a commercial advantage that they can share. It works where both sides have a vested interest in the other's success. We will return to partnership sourcing later, but for now the key issues of it are:

◆ the recognition that the lowest unit purchase price may not give the lowest overall cost.

◆ that suppliers need the confidence of long-term business in order to invest time and money in making the desired improvements.

◆ a commitment to eliminate waste in all its forms in the supply relationship.

◆ balancing the time commitment needed to make the partnership work, recognizing the risk of having a single source of supply.

THE ROLE OF BUYERS

It should be clear by now that a modern purchasing department requires a different buyer approach from that which has been successful in the past.

The traditional role of a buyer has been to react to a purchase request from a user by finding a supply source (often by getting three or four competitive bids), negotiating the terms of the purchase, and handling the administration of the purchase by issuing a purchase order, which can be subsequently matched with a goods received acknowledgment, the original requisition, and an invoice.

Today the buyer's role is much wider. Becoming world class is more about the total company effort in meeting customer needs at a profit, rather than in achieving excellence in individual functional departments.

A key element in achieving this is the integration of the supply chain. The role of the buyer is becoming increasingly one of managing the interface between the supply market and the buyer's own company. This means that the buyer is involved much earlier in the buying process, and is required to monitor supply markets, anticipate trends, and manage suppliers to achieve common goals of better service at lower cost.

Achieving all of these tasks requires specific skills from a buyer. In some cases these will be new skills. They include:

◆ coaching and mentoring skills to bring out the best in your suppliers.

◆ communication and persuasion skills to convey your vision, goals, and plans.

◆ psychology skills to enable you to motivate the different players in your game plan.

◆ financial analysis skills to identify the true costs of your supply channels.

◆ market research skills to monitor your supply markets regularly.

◆ strategy skills to ensure that your goals and objectives mesh with those of the rest of the organization.

SUMMARY

We have learned about the following purchasing issues in this first chapter:

◆ Fundamental changes in business, such as marketing and TQM, have created the need for a new approach to purchasing.

◆ This has led to new tasks for buyers; in particular, the need to focus on more than just price.

◆ The new approach also requires suppliers to adopt a new role, in many cases forming strategic partnerships with their key customers.

◆ This in turn means that buyers have to play a new role—that of supplier manager.

Chapter 2

Objectives and Strategy

In this chapter, we will build on the concepts previously introduced and describe effective strategies for managing different categories of purchase. The way we will do this is to use an approach based on the product portfolio matrix idea developed by Peter Kraljic.

The idea behind the matrix is that management needs to have a supply strategy for its purchases if it is to meet the demands of its end market. This is particularly true when there is a risk of a long-term scarcity due to technological change or economic and political instability around the world. However, not all purchases warrant the investment of the time and effort needed to develop and implement a strategy. Some form of prioritization is needed.

The portfolio matrix approach achieves this prioritization by considering two factors for each purchase—its importance to your company and the complexity of the supply market for that item.

IMPORTANCE OF PURCHASED ITEMS

The first step in the approach is to rank purchased items in order of their importance to your company. There are many factors that can make an item important. The annual spending on the purchased item, of course, is always significant. Some other possibilities are detailed below.

◆ The item is used to make products that may be few in number but that together contribute a major part of your sales and profit.

◆ The item is used to make a large number of your products.

◆ The item is used on a bottleneck resource where failure in availability or quality can potentially stop the entire factory's output.

◆ The item is used in new products that are vital to the future growth of the company.

◆ The cost of nonavailability is high.

If you have a wide range of purchases, then analyzing each one in terms of all these factors may be somewhat daunting. For simplicity, you can use the annual spending on the product expressed as a percentage of the total annual spending on all purchases as a measure of its importance. Further, you can make an arbitrary assumption that if the resulting percentage is less than one, then the item has low importance, and if it is greater than one, its importance is high.

SUPPLY COMPLEXITY

You now need to analyze the supply complexity of each of these products. You need to ask yourself the following questions for each of your supply markets.

◆ Is the product or service in scarce supply?

◆ Is the pace of technological change rapid?

◆ Is it impossible to use an alternative product or service?

◆ Are the barriers for a new supplier to enter the market high?

◆ Are the logistics costs of acquiring the product or service high?

The more *yes* answers given, the more complex the supply market is likely to be.

Another aspect of supply complexity is that of supply risk. There are many types of risk, but the one that causes buyers the most concern is the risk of nonavailability. Different supply markets have different degrees of risk attached to them.

For example, if you buy nuts and bolts of a widely used specification and there are many distributors of these items offering off-the-shelf availability, all within easy geographical reach, then the supply risk is low.

However, if you buy a manufactured part from a supplier who has a six-month lead time, and the supplier is the only one approved by your quality engineers, then the supply risk is high.

A simple way to assess supply complexity is to look at the number of suppliers who are willing and able to supply that product. You may not necessarily buy from all of these suppliers at present. In general, if there are fewer than five such suppliers, the associated risk and complexity is high; if there are more than five, the supply risk and complexity can be considered low.

THE MATRIX

You are now in a position to draw up a portfolio matrix for your purchases. As the illustration shows, there are four quadrants to the matrix, determined by whether their importance and supply complexity is high or low.

		Importance	
		Low	*High*
Complexity	*Low*	**Noncritical** Handle efficiently	**Leverage** Exploit market potential
	High	**Bottleneck** Ensure supply	**Strategic** Cooperate

Noncritical items

These are products or services that are necessary for the smooth running of a company but that in themselves do not represent a major supply risk or have a major impact on the business. The supply risk is low because there are more than five potential suppliers in the marketplace who are both willing and able to supply. The impact is low because they represent less than 1 percent of the total annual purchasing of the company.

The Pareto effect, which states that 80 percent of purchased items typically account for 20 percent of the total budget, means that this category usually has a very large number of small value items. In turn, this means that a buyer can spend a large percentage of his or her time in procuring these items if the same purchasing process is used for everything. In many companies, it is still the practice to obtain three or more quotes before placing an order every time a purchase is required.

Pareto's Law is the theory postulating that the pattern of income distribution is considered constant regardless of any taxation policies. It has also been referred to as law of the trivial many and the critical few, or the *80-20* law. Therefore, if 80 percent a country's income benefits only 20 percent of its population, then the only way to improve the economic condition of the less fortunate is to increase the overall output and income levels. Pareto also created the concept of *Paretian Optimum* that claims resources are optimally distributed when an individual cannot be moved into a better position unless another individual is put in a worse position.

The strategy for noncritical items should be to make the purchasing process as efficient as possible. This may mean negotiating contracts with single sources that are reviewed every year, or every other year, and placing blanket orders that cover all the items bought from that supplier. Users then call in their requirements by telephone, fax, or EDI.

This limits a buyer's involvement to yearly renegotiation of the contract, unless there are problems in delivery or quality during the year. The resulting savings in a buyer's time can be as high as 40 percent, time that can be put to use on more value-added activities.

Other key activities for this category are product standardization and order volume optimization. Product standardization means using as small a range of products as possible to serve the needs of all users. For example, one company used to buy 73 different types of glue for its packaging operation. Close examination of the real needs of the users allowed this to be decreased to just seven different types. Purchasing larger quantities of these seven also meant that the buyer was able to obtain significant price reductions.

Order volume optimization means that when you reorder a product from a supplier, you should look to see if any other products bought from that supplier may need to be ordered soon. If so, by ordering them all at the same time, you may be able to save on costs such as transportation, which more than outweigh any short-term increased inventory holding costs.

Information requirements for the noncritical category of purchases consist of a good overview of the supply markets and good short-term forecasting of requirements. In large purchasing departments these products are generally sourced by junior buyers.

Leverage items

With leverage items, purchasers generally have significant bargaining power with suppliers because the value of purchases is large, and there is a lot of competition in the marketplace due to the large number of potential suppliers.

This bargaining power can be exploited by using spot buying to get the lowest prices, or by working with suppliers on value analysis and cost-reduction projects. If you believe that market prices are going to increase and stay there for a while, you may use your leverage to negotiate longer-term contracts at today's lower prices.

Leverage items require you to have systems in place that give good market and supplier information and allow you to plan your short- and medium-term demands, as well as to forecast price movements. These items are generally the responsibility of senior buying personnel.

Bottleneck items

These items are generally bad news as far as a buyer is concerned. They usually arise due to patents, the need to certify suppliers, or from a specialized technology that is not universally used. There is a potential supply risk because there are few suppliers available, and leverage with the supplier is small because the value of purchases is relatively low.

In the short term, your tactics should be to secure supply by negotiating favorable contracts or investing in inventory. In the longer term, you, and your colleagues in engineering, design, and manufacturing should seek to find alternative products with a wider potential supply base.

You need good medium- to long-term forecasts of demand and good market intelligence. In larger organizations, bottleneck items are the responsibility of higher level management such as the purchasing head.

Strategic items
The key tasks for managing this group of products are:

◆ make or buy decision making.

◆ accurate demand forecasting.

◆ detailed market research.

◆ development of long-term supply relationships.

◆ contingency planning and risk analysis.

You need quite detailed information on supply markets, long-term supply and demand trends, and industry cost curves. The strategic impact that these products can have on your business means that decisions are usually made at a very high level in the organization, such as by the purchasing director.

The strategy and tactics you select largely depend on the relative strengths of the buyer and the supplier. These need to be analyzed very carefully, as explained in the next section.

SUPPLY MARKET ANALYSIS

The next step for the products you have classified as strategic is to assess the supply market systematically in terms of the relative strengths of existing suppliers, and then to compare it with a similar analysis of your bargaining strength. Factors that determine a supplier's strength are:

◆ market size versus the supplier's capacity.

◆ market growth versus the supplier's capacity growth.

◆ supplier's capacity utilization.

◆ profitability of the supplier.

◆ supplier's cost and price structure.

◆ level at which the supplier breaks even.

◆ uniqueness of the product and the stability of the technology used.

◆ entry barriers, either know-how or capital, for companies wishing to enter the market.

In contrast, factors that make a buyer strong include:

◆ purchase volume versus capacity of main suppliers.

◆ demand growth versus capacity growth.

◆ capacity utilization of main suppliers.

◆ market share compared to main competition.

◆ profitability of main products.

◆ production capability for making the purchased product.

◆ cost and price structure.

One way to measure the relative strengths is to use a scoring system for each of the factors mentioned. This can be a rating from, say, 1 to 5. The total score is then an indication of strength. For example:

◆ less than 10   = low strength

◆ 11 to 20   = medium strength

◆ more than 20 = high strength

You can then compare your bargaining position with each of your suppliers using the following matrix.

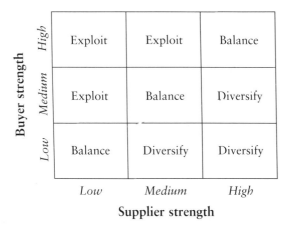

		Low	Medium	High
Buyer strength	*High*	Exploit	Exploit	Balance
	Medium	Exploit	Balance	Diversify
	Low	Balance	Diversify	Diversify
		Low	*Medium*	*High*

Supplier strength

This comparison shows which of three basic strategic thrusts are available. For items where you dominate the market and the supplier's strength is low to medium, you should try to exploit your advantage by negotiating favorable prices and contract terms. Even so, you should be careful not to jeopardize long-term relationships, or to provoke countermeasures that may in the end prove costly.

Where suppliers are much stronger than you, you need to adopt a more defensive strategy. This means taking steps to ensure supply in the short term, for example, by building up strategic stocks while you search for substitute products. In other words, diversifying from your current product.

If the comparison shows that there is a balance of strength with your suppliers, you need to adopt a strategy that is not too defensive and costly, but that at the same time is not overly aggressive and damaging to supplier relationships.

Much of your company's cash is sitting in a back room. It is known as inventory or stock. You need to know how to improve the management of that inventory so that it yields even more profit. Space translates into money, and if you have merchandise taking up valuable room in your warehouse because it's not being sold quickly enough, it is costing you. You must watch this inventory closely so that you keep those items that customers need and demand, and reduce items that are not moving.

Here are some ways to improve your operation and increase inventory turnover:

◆ Stock items according to how profitable they are. What you want to do is have your best-selling items in sufficient quantity. Customers generally are not willing to wait for back orders.

◆ Modernize your inventory by using bar codes and computer-aided systems. Updated inventory controls enable you to keep better track of your stock.

◆ Use a practical delivery schedule with suppliers. Some businesses have the supplier visit them on a regular basis to determine what needs to be replenished.

◆ Replace old with new. Keep up to date on industry developments. Get rid of outdated, outmoded items.

◆ Reduce the reserve stock. More and more companies today are cutting back on items kept in reserve. In fact, many companies now stock items on a consignment basis, which allows them to return the merchandise if they find it can't be moved fast enough.

SUMMARY

This chapter explained how to build a strategy for procuring goods and services that allows you to formulate and prioritize plans for managing your supply base. The key steps are:

◆ Rank all purchases in terms of their importance to the company.

◆ Assess the complexity of the marketplace for these purchases, paying particular attention to supply risk.

◆ Based on their importance and supply complexity, decide whether each purchase is noncritical, bottleneck, leverage, or strategic, and adopt the appropriate strategy and tactics.

◆ For the strategic items, compare your bargaining strength with that of your suppliers and decide whether to exploit your position, diversify from that product, or follow a balanced strategy.

Chapter 3

Deciding
What to Buy

In deciding what to buy, there are three things that you need to determine.

The first question you have to answer is whether you should buy the goods from external sources or make it yourselves. This question should also be asked of services that you propose contracting out, and is called a make-or-buy decision.

Second, you need to prepare some kind of description of the items that you do have to purchase from suppliers. This is called a specification and is a key statement in ensuring that suppliers understand and deliver exactly what you need.

The third item that you have to consider is how to decide when to purchase and in what quantity. This is not always as easy and straightforward as it appears.

MAKE-OR-BUY DECISIONS

One of the roles of the buyer is to review all potential sources of supply and to select suppliers who will give the lowest overall cost. Too often, we think of this activity purely in terms of external suppliers. However, for some goods or services, your own company may be capable of providing what you want. The comparison between using your own company as a supplier and using a third party is a make-or-buy decision.

The factors that shape the make-or-buy decision are

1. the relative costs of making or buying the item or service.

2. the capacity situation of the company.

3. the future supply market.

Relative costs

The easiest way to explain the relative cost side of the make-or-buy equation is to look at a simple example. Suppose your accountant has estimated the cost per unit of your company producing a part and it looks like this:

	$
Direct material	15
Direct labor	5
Variable overhead	2
Fixed overhead	6
Total cost	28

You discover from your supply market research that the same item can be bought on the open market for $25. Should you make it or buy it?

It seems like you should buy it because to do so appears to be $3 cheaper. However, if you think about the before and after situations of producing it yourselves, you get a different picture.

	If you make the part $	If you don't make the part $
Direct material	15	0
Direct labor	5	0
Variable overhead	2	0
Fixed overhead	6	6
Total cost	28	6

The difference between making the part yourselves and not making it yourselves is really $22. This is because the fixed costs of production are there whether you make anything or not. The incremental cost to you is really the direct variable costs and these should be the only ones considered. On this basis, it is cheaper to make the part yourselves than to buy it from a supplier.

Capacity considerations

It is all very well if you have sufficient capacity to make the volume of the part you want. What if you don't have sufficient capacity? In that case, you have to calculate what contribution to fixed overhead and profit you would have earned if you hadn't been making this new part. This then becomes an opportunity cost that you must include in the overall cost calculation.

Future supply conditions

In addition to the quantitative aspects of calculating the relative costs of making or buying the part, there are other considerations that are more qualitative and subjective.

For example, if you decide to source the part or service with an external supplier, is the future supply market likely to be reliable? The analyses from your portfolio matrix will help in this but you will need market research systems to help continually review the situation.

What is the likely stability of prices in the future? Your decision to source the part externally has been made on the basis of current prices. Will prices increase faster than internal manufacturing costs and will this change the decision? Sensitivity analyses at the decision-making stage will help you determine the price range in which the decision remains the correct one.

PURCHASE DESCRIPTIONS

A description of what the user wants has to be relayed to suppliers, often via the purchasing department. Unless there is a way of making sure that the message of what is wanted is not distorted, there is a risk that suppliers will misinterpret your requirements.

One mechanism for providing clear and unambiguous messages of what is required is the purchase specification, commonly known as specs. Specification (*specs*) is a description or detailed instruction provided in conjunction with product plans or a purchase order. Specifications may stipulate the type of materials to be used, dimensions, colors, qualities, and characteristics of a product. There are three basic types of specs:

◆ commercial

◆ design

◆ performance

◆ TQM

Commercial specifications

These are specifications produced by a specific governing body. They set standards for the quality of materials used, the quality of workmanship involved in production, as well as for such items as critical dimensions, chemical composition, and allowable tolerances.

Nuts, bolts, and chemicals are the kind of items often covered by a commercial specification. They are all items with a wide application, so manufacturers can plan production with the confidence that there will be a large demand. This confidence allows them to have long production runs that give them high efficiencies and low costs. These costs can then be passed on in the form of low prices, which is one reason for specifying a product with a commercial specification whenever possible.

Design specifications

If the cost of the standard item is unacceptable, or if there is a supply risk because the product is protected by patent or copyright, it may be worthwhile to develop your own specification in order to increase the potential supply base.

However, the danger in doing this is that you may produce a specification that is too detailed. This may incur unnecessary cost because it does not allow suppliers to use their expertise in producing it. It may also mean that the buyer unintentionally assumes all responsibility for the performance of the purchased part. For example, if you specify that a dimension has to have a tolerance of

+/–0.01 inch when, in fact, it should be +/–0.005 inch, then the responsibility is yours.

Performance specifications

Performance specifications avoid the drawbacks of design specifications by specifying in detail the performance required, but *not* the method of achieving that performance. In this way, suppliers are free to choose the materials they use and the manufacturing process they employ. Giving suppliers this leeway should result in lower costs because you are allowing them to use their expertise in producing the item.

TQM

Total quality management (TQM) is a concept developed by W. Edwards Deming. It encompasses 14 points and is a philosophy whereby the central focus is continual quality improvement achieved through company-wide cooperation and bolstered by ongoing employee training. Deming rejects performance reviews and work quotas and believes in reinstituting individual employee pride of workmanship.

WHEN TO BUY

The timing of the purchase decision for many one-time purchases such as office equipment, training, and cars is relatively straightforward. If a budget has been agreed on with management and the financing is available, the timing of the purchase is dictated by the user's need for the purchased item.

The timing of the purchase decision for repeat purchases, such as direct production materials and consumables, is more complicated. Factors that complicate the decision-making process include:

◆ the quantity you currently possess compared with the quantity you need in the near future.

◆ the lead time between issuing an order to a supplier and receiving the goods.

◆ any minimum order for purchases from the supplier.

◆ the requirements for other products you buy from the same supplier, which may be desirable to order at the same time to reduce transportation costs.

MAINTAINING STOCK

In many companies these considerations often result in the decision to keep some stock of the item to ensure availability when needed. The question then is, how much stock should be kept?

The answer to this lies in the diagram here, which shows the fundamentals of a stock system, commonly referred to as a reorder point system. In this system, stock eventually reaches a level called the reorder point (ROP) at which an order is issued to the supplier. (The reorder point is the minimum level of inventory that is tolerated; at that point, a new order must be placed. The reorder point considers the time delay in receiving new inventory, the typical rate of inventory consumption, and the stockout cost.)

The standard supply lead time (L) is the usual time taken between the order being issued and the buyer receiving the goods.

During this lead time, the buying company uses, on average, D units of the part. The risk to the buying company is that usage for the part will be greater than D during the lead time and that they will, therefore, run out before the order arrives. As a result, it is common practice to keep a safety stock (S), which will cover some of this above-average usage. The average amount in stock is the safety stock plus half the reorder quantity (Q).

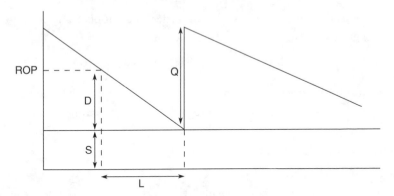

Timing decisions for items controlled by a reorder point system are then made semiautomatically, in that the system will recommend that an order be placed when the current on-hand stock falls below the reorder point. Buyers should review these suggestions and amend as necessary, based on their knowledge of current supplier performance and their company's needs.

Bar coding once was used solely by supermarkets. No more. It is now an inventory process in almost every kind of business, from shoe stores to employment agencies to tire manufacturers. If you have to count and keep track of various items in inventory, the progress of goods in the manufacturing process, or any vast number of files, then bar coding may be essential for your company.

A bar code is basically a printed pattern of wide and narrow bars that contain the coding for data such as an item's price, its warehouse location, or its date of manufacture. A computer reads the bar code by optically scanning it with a laser beam or with a wand that contains a light source and a photocell. The bars are converted into data that the computer stores and analyzes.

Bar coding gives a company an accurate, running list of its inventory and sales. This allows better monitoring of the company's needs and increases its ability to reorder more efficiently based on that need. It allows instantaneous monitoring of the manufacturing process.

Bar coding is particularly important when dealing with fixed asset physical inventories because it allows the company to obtain large amounts of information quickly, accurately, and cost effectively. For instance, a physical inventory of a medium-sized company could involve 10,000 assets. To get information on each asset using manual means could take an inordinate amount of time. In addition, the people taking the inventory—the counters—are prone to a much higher degree of error.

You start first with a bar code label. There are many bar code labeling systems in use today, so only minor modifications may be necessary to design one for your particular needs. Also, a number of industries already have a bar code standard in place, and you only have to adapt what was previously designed.

Investments in a bar coding system generally pay back in six months to two years. All the costs of the present system (including time, labor, staffing, and equipment) must be calculated against the costs involved in implementing a bar code system, including direct costs (equipment, supplies, and reduced staffing) and indirect costs (reduced errors and improved response time).

IMPROVING STOCK PERFORMANCE

Once the reorder report system for placing orders with suppliers is working efficiently, you can turn your attention to improving its performance. There are three things you can do to reduce the amount of stock needed for a given level of availability.

1. Improve forecasts.

2. Reduce supplier lead times.

3. Reduce purchase quantities.

Improving forecasts

The more accurate the forecast, the less safety stock you will need to carry to buffer production from uncertainties in requirements.

The first step is to choose an appropriate statistical method for forecasting. Most forecasting methods are based on the assumption that demand for a product in the immediate future will bear some kind of relationship to that shown in the past. A simple way of forecasting based on this assumption is to use a moving average. More sophisticated systems using exponential smoothing techniques give a more robust result, but are correspondingly more difficult to use and interpret.

Reducing supplier lead times

Reducing supplier lead times has two benefits for stock holding. The first is that the shorter the lead time, the less safety stock you need to hold to allow for uncertainties in demand during the lead time.

The second benefit is that the shorter the lead time, the shorter the horizon over which you need to forecast. This should mean that forecasts are more accurate, which in turn means that you need to hold less stock.

Reducing purchase quantities

The second component of stock holding is the purchase quantity. Any quantity that is greater than your immediate requirements goes into stock. The greater the quantity purchased at any one time, the more that will have to be stored for future use and the greater the average stock holding.

The traditional way to calculate the correct quantity to purchase is to use the economic order quantity formula.

The major problem with this is that it accepts the need for costs and merely trades one type of cost for another. A much better approach is to work with suppliers to find ways of making it cost-effective to deliver a quantity of just one, if that is all that is required.

MATERIALS REQUIREMENTS PLANNING

Reorder point systems, such as the one just described, are fine for products that have what is called independent demand. In other words, the sale or usage of that product is not determined by the sale or usage of another product.

However, this is not generally the case for materials or products used in a manufacturing process. For example, a manufacturer of bicycles knows that for every bicycle he makes he will need two wheels. The demand for wheels is determined by the number of bicycles he plans to make. Wheels are then said to have dependent demand.

The problem in using reorder point systems for dependent demand items is that the probability of having all the components you need when you need them falls with the increase in the number of components used. Unless you are prepared to hold very high levels of stock of components, which is expensive, you may not be able to meet all manufacturing's requirements.

A more effective way of planning purchases to meet manufacturing's needs is to use a system called materials requirements planning. This uses manufacturing's master production schedule, or MPS, as its starting point. The MPS identifies the products and their quantities that will be manufactured in each week or month for the next six to twelve months.

The MPS is then "exploded" into a list of all the components that will be needed to manufacture the MPS requirements and the dates on which they will be used. Knowing the supply lead times for the components allows buyers to schedule purchases from suppliers so that the correct quantities are received by the required date.

The result is that buyers can meet the demand from their manufacturing departments and at the same time keep little or no stock of their own.

JUST-IN-TIME SUPPLY

Another book in this series looks at Just-in-Time manufacturing and the dramatic effect it can have on a company's performance. Just-in-Time (JIT) inventory control is a method of close coordination with suppliers that maximizes the relationship between production and sales levels with inventory, thereby reducing carrying costs. Often, JIT is linked with a computerized point-of-sale system with inventory levels maintained via an automated reordering system connected to suppliers. As a result, stockouts are minimized.

The next logical step is to use the JIT philosophy to schedule purchases with suppliers. The target is to develop a network of suppliers who can consistently deliver quantities that exactly match your immediate production requirements, at the time when you need them (not too early or too late) while meeting your quality standards every time. This will allow you to reduce your stock holding dramatically, and at the same time be more responsive to your customers' needs.

The key, of course, to turning out consistently defect-free products is to focus not on the products themselves but rather on the processes that create them. In a JIT manufacturing facility, every operator has access to a switch that can halt the entire production line. Whenever a defect is discovered, the operator can immediately shut down the line. All these operators assemble as a team to figure out how the defect occurred. They then modify the process to ensure that the defect does not recur. This new approach has been highly successful and is now embraced by most manufacturers.

SUMMARY

This chapter looked at ways of deciding what items you should buy from outside your organization and methods for deciding when to buy.

The first consideration was whether you could provide the item or service more economically from within your own organization. This led to looking at make-or-buy decisions and at how to calculate the relevant costs.

We next looked at the importance of product descriptions in making sure that the supplier knows exactly what you want, and that you are buying the most cost-effective means of meeting your needs.

We then looked at methods for deciding when to buy. These were:

◆ stock holding systems that trigger an order when a certain stock level is reached.

◆ materials requirement planning systems that allow you to meet requirements with less stock by forecasting demand accurately.

◆ Just-in-Time systems that trigger supplies on very short lead times to meet immediate requirements.

Chapter 4

Selecting and Managing Suppliers

The key to achieving purchasing objectives of service at the lowest cost is the way in which you select, manage, and develop your suppliers. The major tasks for buyers in doing this effectively are:

◆ researching and monitoring both current and potential sources of supply.

◆ addressing the strategic and tactical issues in selecting suppliers.

◆ coordinating the inputs from the rest of the organization in supplier selection.

◆ developing and controlling a plan to manage suppliers.

RESEARCHING THE SUPPLY BASE

Many information sources are available to buyers these days that enable them to identify potential suppliers of a product or service. A few of the most commonly used sources are:

◆ your own company's database of current and past suppliers.

◆ trade directories.

◆ telephone Yellow Pages.

◆ trade press.

◆ suppliers themselves—either visits from the salesforce or other supplier initiatives such as direct mail.

◆ exhibitions and conferences.

◆ chambers of commerce.

◆ the trade section of foreign embassies for information on global
   sources.

From these, you can draw up a list of potential suppliers. However,
you will also need to monitor your key markets continually for
trends and events that may have an impact on your initial choice of
supplier or even trigger the need to look for new suppliers.

In addition to the sources of information on current and potential
suppliers, other sources of information useful for monitoring supply markets include:

◆ company annual reports.

◆ market research firms that undertake research for themselves
   and then make it available to others at a reasonable price.

◆ suppliers' sales forces.

◆ your employees.

◆ supplier advertising in the press. For example, recruitment advertising can give an indication of the supplier's expansion plans.

STRATEGIC AND TACTICAL ISSUES

Before final selection of a supplier, there are several strategic and tactical issues you need to agree on with your management team.

Early supplier involvement

The experience of many companies has been that involving suppliers at an early stage in the development of their products can produce significant advantages. The areas in which suppliers can help include:

◆ setting specifications.

◆ agreeing upon tolerances.

◆ suggesting opportunities for standardization.

◆ process and assembly improvements.

◆ packaging.

◆ inventory management.

◆ transportation.

Colleagues need to agree to, and be aware of, early supplier involvement because you need the suppliers' input before the design of a new product is frozen. Many companies only think about suppliers after the design has been set.

Early supplier involvement is an approach that is usually appropriate for certain products within the strategic and leverage areas of the product portfolio.

Single or multisource?

Whether to have a policy of using a single or using two or more sources for added security is a thorny issue for many companies, but there is no clear-cut reason to opt for one choice or the other.

In general, your strategy towards single or multisourcing should be determined by a product's position in your portfolio. Noncritical parts should be single sourced, as the cost of administering a large supply base usually outweighs any of the benefits of multisourcing.

Leverage products can be a mixture of single and multisourced depending on whether you are using your leverage in these markets to secure long-term supply at advantageous prices, or are aiming to get low average prices from spot buying.

For bottleneck products, you should try to secure supply in the short term. This may mean placing contracts with more than one supplier, if more than one is available, or negotiating a contract on favorable terms with just one supplier.

The same considerations apply to strategic products as for bottleneck products. Sharing your requirements on, say, a 60/40 basis with two suppliers may reduce your supply risk. This is particularly true if the balance of negotiating power lies with you.

Share of business

Buyers should always look to improve their negotiating position with suppliers. One way of doing this is to increase the volume of trade placed with them. Of course, the danger with this approach is that it can result in your business accounting for a very high percentage of their output. If you then decide to switch suppliers, it can have a devastating impact on the original company, even to the point of putting it out of business.

This is a moral dilemma in which few companies would consciously wish to find themselves. Indeed, many of the larger companies now have a policy of not taking more than, say, 30 percent of any supplier's output. However, adopting such a policy can mean that you have to dual or multisource some products.

Local, national, or global sourcing?

With modern communications and transportation, it is now much easier to source products from further afield. One decision you have to make is whether to source a product locally, nationally, or even internationally. The advantages of local sourcing include the following.

◆ Cooperation is better because it is easier to visit each other and sort out problems or attack opportunities.

◆ Transportation is a small part of the overall lead time for procurement, so stocks can be reduced. In fact, this is a prerequisite of JIT supply.

◆ Emergency orders are more easily met.

◆ It helps to support the local community and thus increases the company's public image.

The advantages of buying nationally come from the fact that national suppliers tend to be bigger than local suppliers. Here are some of the advantages.

◆ Economies of scale get passed on to us in the form of lower prices.

◆ National suppliers may be able to offer better technical assistance.

◆ They may be able to meet any fluctuations in demand because of their larger capacity.

◆ Shortages are less likely to occur.

The major reason that many companies now look to world markets for key purchases is lower prices. This price difference can more than offset the increased cost of sourcing overseas. However, there are potentially significant risks attached to overseas sourcing. These include:

◆ the length of the supply line, which makes it difficult for suppliers to react to changes in requirements.

◆ increased inventory to safeguard availability, given that lead times tend to be longer and more variable, particularly if the goods are transported by sea.

◆ exposure to currency fluctuations.

Manufacturer or distributor?

In some instances, you may have the option of sourcing products with either the manufacturer or one of its authorized distributors. An advantage of sourcing directly with the manufacturer is that you cut out the middleman and so should pay less.

However, distributors may offer a service that the manufacturer is not willing to provide, such as technical support and after-sales service. This is increasingly a factor when buying personal computers and peripheral equipment, for example.

Also, distributors often deal in product lines from more than one manufacturer. You may find that you can concentrate your purchases with one distributor and use the leverage to get lower overall prices. Office stationery is one example where it can make sense to deal with a distributor rather than the individual manufacturers.

SELECTING SUPPLIERS

Many departments within the company have an interest in which suppliers are chosen. Each has a different view on what makes a supplier a good one. Some of these views are qualitative, others are quantitative. Your task is to channel these different views into a coherent and consistent method for selecting suppliers that produces the best supplier base to meet your company's objectives.

The type of supplier evaluation you should implement depends on the nature of the product you are buying. You should use only a basic form of evaluation on products in the noncritical quadrant of your product portfolio in order to minimize the cost of evaluation. Items in the bottleneck and strategic quadrants need a more rigorous approach, and it pays to make this evaluation a team effort. Suppliers of leverage products may or may not be given a rigorous evaluation depending on your strategy towards them.

Preliminary evaluation

You can make preliminary evaluations by using a mixture of desk research and a mailing to potential suppliers asking for information. The information you need to gather includes:

◆ product range.

◆ production capacity in total and current utilization.

◆ quality standards achieved, such as ISO 9000.

◆ financial performance.

◆ credit rating, such as that awarded by Dun and Bradstreet.

◆ customer referrals.

Follow-up evaluation

Now that you have a smaller list of potential suppliers, the next step is to investigate them in more detail. This is usually done by your team visiting their premises and carrying out an audit of their activities. The audit should cover:

◆ financial stability.

◆ ability to do the work.

◆ capacity to do the work.

◆ understanding of your needs.

In addition, you need to assess them in terms of what they are like to deal with as people. This is important as many problems and opportunities depend on the way you work together as a team.

You should use a standard document in making this assessment so the team is consistent in the way that it evaluates different companies. It will also aid later comparisons between competing suppliers. A simple example is shown on page 51. In practice, you may need to evaluate much more than this.

Supplier Evaluation Form

Rate the supplier on a scale of 0 to 5 for each of the categories below. The evaluation ratings should be interpreted as follows:

1 = poor and could not be improved in the short term
2 = poor but could be improved with considerable effort
3 = meets the standard required in most aspects
4 = meets the standard required in all respects
5 = exceeds the standard in all respects

Supplier attitude
- willingness to respond to your needs
- ability to respond to your needs
- quality of consultation on new product development
- quality of market information supplied
- initiatives in cost reduction measures

Technical ability
- technical competence
- process capability
- process control

Commercial
- lead time
- supplier location
- delivery frequency
- minimum order quantities
- percent of order schedules filled on time
- supply risk
- purchase price

Financial
- credit terms
- credit rating
- key financial ratios

Bear in mind when conducting these visits that they are an opportunity for you to sell your company to the supplier. This can be important if you are much smaller than the supplier and you need to ensure the supply of products in the strategic or bottleneck areas.

ISO

One of the buzzwords for business quality has become ISO, which stands for International Organization for Standardization. It represents a system of quality control standards to measure businesses. Specifically, it is called ISO 9000 and consists of five subdivisions of requirements for developing and operating a system whose intent is to give assurance that the product provides what the customer wants and expects.

It was developed in Europe about 20 years ago by a Geneva-based group representing the standard-setting bodies of some 90 countries and governmental organizations. However, it was not established in the United States until 1987 when Ford Motor Company boosted profits by an astounding 40 percent, which it achieved by controlling its processes to meet a minimum set of customer expectations.

ISO 9000 is a set of guidelines for a standard operating procedure that applies on a worldwide basis. A company develops the system for its product by applying these guidelines. The standard itself focuses on 20 elements in a quality program. Each relates to a specific aspect of satisfying customers. These include management responsibility, design control, document and data control, product identification and traceability, inspection and testing, corrective and preventive action, internal quality audits, and servicing.

MANAGING AND DEVELOPING SUPPLIERS

A well-motivated and responsive supplier base is a valuable asset to any company. This is particularly true in high technology industries or where there is potential for scarcity of key raw materials.

Such a supplier base is achieved by developing goodwill through the way you manage and develop your suppliers. It means being completely open, impartial, and fair at all times. If achieved, goodwill can encourage suppliers to invest time and effort in understanding your business and its problems, and to work with you to find solutions.

The potential for improving company performance in this way is so great that many companies have decided to form partnerships with their key suppliers. The key steps to achieving partnerships are as follows:

Step 1—Deciding on the markets and products

The first step is to review company strategy. This will help you decide on the sort of suppliers you need in order to achieve your corporate objectives concerning company size, new products, and key markets. Using the portfolio matrix analysis you performed earlier, you can identify the strategic products that would benefit from partnership sourcing. You can then develop an action plan based on this strategic review of products and markets to put forward to the rest of your organization.

Step 2—Selling the idea

As with any major initiative, support from top management is vital. The action plan you developed from your strategic analysis will help you communicate the benefits to be gained as a result of improved quality and service and a reduction in total cost.

You also need to sell the concept to other departments in your company. Many of these will either help or obstruct your efforts to introduce partnership sourcing. For example, accounts payable needs to pay suppliers on time and production needs to communicate changes in their plans that affect suppliers.

Finally, you need to sell the idea to your key suppliers. You need to stress the benefits to them of: stability due to long-term contracts; lower costs from such areas as better planning and design, simplified logistics, and cooperative cost reduction projects; and strategic advantages, such as access to your technology, shared problem solving, and management input.

Step 3—Choosing your first partners

First, you need to define the parameters for selecting partners. These include many of the factors on your supplier evaluation form. You can then review your current suppliers' performance against these parameters for evidence that they could be good partners.

Step 4—Define what you both want from the partnership

You will need to develop a style of working together with which both sides feel comfortable. Much of this is intangible and cannot be measured, covering things like trust, commitment, flexibility, teamwork, and persistence. Practical tools to help foster the working relationship include the use of continuous improvement teams, open-book accounting, and continuous assessment.

If partnerships are to work, they must have tangible objectives that both sides agree upon. These must be defined at the start of the partnership and targets and plans set for their accomplishment. They include topics such as:

◆ total costs.

◆ total quality management.

◆ zero defects.

◆ joint research and development.

◆ faster time to market.

◆ JIT deliveries.

Step 5—Making the partnership work
Partnerships do not work by themselves. You must have a process for monitoring progress, resolving problems as they occur, and communicating the results so as to build commitment and enthusiasm for the project. Here are some ways to do this.

◆ Set up a joint review team that meets regularly. This team is responsible for monitoring progress and making sure the project meets its deadlines. It is also responsible for resourcing problem-solving teams to attack the major issues.

◆ Implement systems for monitoring and measuring progress. These should measure progress to agreed targets on criteria such as on-time deliveries, lead times, service levels, and failure rates.

◆ Build the relationship through activities such as sharing business plans, joint research and development, and sharing technology.

SUMMARY

In this chapter, we have concentrated on how to select and manage suppliers for peak performance. The key steps are:

◆ thorough research of potential sources of supply.

◆ addressing the strategic and tactical issues around the sort of supply base required.

◆ selection of suppliers using a rigorous evaluation process that allows different suppliers to be compared fairly.

◆ the implementation of a supply partnership agreement for key suppliers.

Chapter 5

Determining the Price

This is perhaps the most crucial aspect of purchasing. Any reduction in the purchase price paid will show in the accounts of the company as an equal increase in profits. Hence, the pressure is on buyers to get the lowest price possible.

No one would argue against this in principle. However, there are other costs to bear in mind when purchasing goods and services. Typical sources of additional cost for many companies include:

- purchasing systems for generating purchase requisitions, orders, acknowledgments, and processing supplier invoices.

- material handling costs for unloading, storing, and moving goods that are not required immediately.

- checking the supplier by counting goods received, issuing receiving reports, inspecting the quality of goods received, and sorting the good ones from the bad ones.

- poor quality resulting in scrap, rework, or return transportation to the supplier.

Therefore, the buyer's task is to reduce the overall cost, not just the purchase price.

PURCHASE PRICE

Getting the right price can mean the difference between success and failure for many companies. What constitutes the right price can change over time and so the approach to pricing must be continually reviewed. An understanding of the factors that contribute to this decision-making process is vital.

Cost behavior

In the long run, all companies must recover all their costs if they are to stay in business. There are three major categories of cost.

Variable costs: these are costs that vary with the volume of product or service provided. For example, raw materials in a manufacturing company are a variable cost. If production is increased, the cost of raw materials will increase in direct proportion to the increased volume of product produced. Equally, if production is reduced, raw material costs will reduce in proportion.

Fixed costs: these are costs that have to be paid even if production is zero. Labor costs in a service organization are a good example of a fixed cost as is the cost of rent in a manufacturing company. Fixed costs tend to vary with time rather than volume of production, within certain limits.

Semivariable costs: some costs are neither purely variable or purely fixed. An example of this is maintenance costs. This consists of planned maintenance, the fixed element, which is undertaken no matter what the level of production activity, and unplanned maintenance, such as repairs, which varies in proportion to the level of production.

However, in the short term, companies may be prepared to accept a price that just recovers the variable element of their costs. A knowledge of costs and cost behavior for companies in your supply market can give you an edge in negotiations.

A useful tool for analyzing company costs is break-even analysis. This is a chart that shows how the costs of a company change with different volumes of output. The accompanying diagram shows just such an analysis. One can be constructed for any supplier by performing these steps:

1. On a sheet of paper, draw a horizontal line to represent the range of output of the company from 0 to 100 percent.

2. Take the total sales value ($20 million in your example) from the firm's latest annual accounts and plot this value on the vertical axis of the graph. On the horizontal axis plot the normal operating output of the company for the period covered by the annual accounts (in your example, this is 80 percent). It is unlikely that you will be able to get an accurate figure for this, unless your supplier tells you. You will need to use your judgment and experience from visiting the supplier to gauge what this is likely to be. Mark on the graph where these two values intersect.

3. Draw a straight line from 0 to the point just plotted, and extend it to the limit of the chart (i.e., to 100 percent).

4. Again from the annual accounts, take the value of fixed costs and locate this on the vertical axis. Starting from this point, draw a horizontal line across the graph.

5. Take the total cost (in your example $15 million) from the annual accounts and mark where this value intersects with the operating level you used previously (80 percent).

6. Draw a line between the start of the fixed cost line and this point and extend it to the limit of the graph.

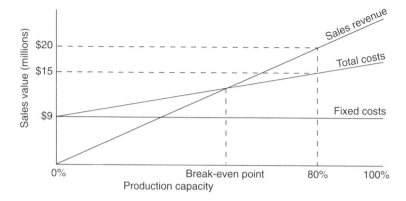

The break-even point is the point at which the total cost line intersects the total sales line. The corresponding value on the horizontal axis is the capacity at which the company must operate in order to break even. Operating at a level above this, the company makes a profit. Below it, the company makes a loss.

It must be stressed that the accuracy of this approach is dependent on the accuracy of the data used to construct it. The cost data available to buyers from published sources, such as annual accounts, will be aggregate data for the company as a whole and not for a particular product. Consequently, the approach works best in process industries where companies tend to have small product ranges. Nevertheless, it is a useful source of information to employ with suppliers in negotiations.

Suppliers' pricing behavior

Different companies have different priorities and strategies when it comes to pricing their product range. A knowledge of this enables the enterprising buyer to use his or her market and cost knowledge for the best effect when negotiating prices.

For a start, most companies do not sell just one product but a range of products. They do not necessarily expect to make the same profit margin on all. Indeed, if they do price products in such a way that all products earn the same margin, then the most efficiently produced products will be overpriced. This can be used as a lever to obtain reductions on some items in the range.

Similarly, many companies do not expect all customers to earn them the same level of profit. You should use your leverage to make sure that your company is one of the low margin customers.

Modifying the price

Most companies modify their prices to encourage certain types of behavior. For example, a discount may be given for early payment. This reduces the supplier's collection costs and potential bad debt costs, as well as improving liquidity.

A quantity discount for buying a large volume is another way that a supplier can reduce the costs involved in selling, storing inventory, and transportation.

Functional discounts (also called trade discounts) are given to customers who, in return, perform some service in the supply channel, such as selling, storing, or record keeping.

Seasonal discounts are sometimes given in situations where demand for a product varies with the time of year. By offering a lower price out of season, sales volume can be increased and so production is kept at a more constant level.

PRICING ANALYSIS

It is clear that with all these factors potentially influencing the price of a product, you must perform some kind of price analysis for every purchase made. Four tools can be used as an aid in this analysis.

◆ competitive bidding

◆ comparison with market prices

◆ comparison with historical prices

◆ target pricing

Competitive bidding

This form of price comparison is normally used in situations where the following six conditions exist.

1. The value of the purchase is high enough to justify the cost involved for both the buyer and the seller in preparing and analyzing the invitation to bid and the subsequent bid.

2. The specification of the purchased item or service is explicitly clear to both the buyer and the seller.

3. There are an adequate number of suppliers who are both willing and able to supply.

4. There is sufficient time for the buyer to prepare the invitation and for potential suppliers to produce a well-thought-out and documented bid.

5. It is possible for suppliers to estimate the costs involved with a high degree of precision.

6. It is not anticipated that changes will need to be made to the specification at a later date. Otherwise a supplier may bid low in order to get the contract and when locked in to it, make a larger profit from later alterations to the specification.

If these conditions exist then the lowest bid usually represents a fair and reasonable price. However, a buyer should not conduct the bidding process in a mechanical fashion. As with all price analysis and negotiation, common sense should be used and the resulting price compared with other benchmarks such as the price paid in the past for a similar piece of work.

Comparison with market prices

Where there are many suppliers of a product or service, competition and the laws of supply and demand usually result in a fair price. This is generally true if the product is a standard one. If there is any basis on which the product or service can be differentiated from competitors, then the supplier may charge, and possibly get, a premium price. One role of the professional buyer is to question the need for the differentiated product and seek to get agreement to use a standard product that costs less but provides the same core functions.

Comparison with historic prices

Comparing the current price with that paid in the past for the same or similar item can give an indication of the reasonableness of the price. However, you must always question whether conditions have changed since the last purchase was made and if so, whether historic price is now a fair one to use for comparison purposes.

Target pricing

Target pricing is used when price analysis is impractical or does not allow the buyer to arrive at the conclusion that the price is reasonable. It can also be used to identify the major cost components of a purchase as a basis for working with suppliers on cost reduction projects.

The first step is to obtain a cost breakdown of the purchased item or service. Many buyers now require their suppliers to provide this as part of the bidding process or as part of the commitment to partnership sourcing. If you cannot obtain such a breakdown directly from the supplier, an alternative way is to produce your own using in-house experts. This latter way of identifying the different elements of purchase cost is sometimes called reverse engineering. The resulting analysis should look something like this example.

		$
Direct material	*20lb @ $6/lb*	*120*
Less scrap	*5%*	*6*
Net direct material cost		*114*
Purchased components		*107*
Total material cost		*221*
Direct labor	*3 hours @ $10/hour*	*30*
Variable production costs		*251*
Fixed production costs		*105*
Other fixed costs		*180*
Total costs		*536*
Selling price		*600*
Profit		*64 or 10.7%*

You can use your knowledge, or that of your colleagues in engineering and production, to review whether these individual costs are fair.

LEARNING AND EXPERIENCE CURVES

Researchers have shown that in some industries labor costs are reduced as the total volume of production increases. In addition, they have shown that these costs are reduced in a predictable manner. The relationship between costs and volume is called a learning curve.

A learning curve is usually described in terms of the percentage cost reduction achieved by each doubling of production. So, for example, a 30 percent learning curve means that costs are reduced by 30 percent each time production is doubled. This is understandable, as you would expect the labor force to become more efficient and skilled at carrying out a complicated task the more times they do it.

Learning curve reductions relate to direct labor costs. In a similar way, total costs fall as volume increases due to organizational improvements brought about by management. Examples of this are material cost reduction through product redesign, and manufacturing efficiencies brought about by process improvements.

The importance of these concepts to the buyer is that they can be used as aids in target pricing analysis to judge whether current prices are fair, and also as a basis for agreeing on future cost-reduction targets.

NEGOTIATIONS

As we have seen, the price that a seller ideally wants can be modified in a number of ways. The question for buyers is how to go about modifying the price to get it as low as possible, without affecting other considerations such as logistics costs and the quality of service needed.

One way is to use competitive bidding and to rely on competition to drive the price down. This is not always practical and does not necessarily get the best result.

Another way is to enter into a negotiation with selected suppliers. The hallmarks of a good negotiation are that it:

◆ produces a result that is fair to both parties.

◆ is efficient in terms of the time taken and resources used to reach the agreement.

◆ improves, or at least does not damage, the relationship between buyer and seller.

Too often, however, a typical negotiation starts with the seller stating the price and conditions wanted, and then the buyer putting in a counterbid. The negotiation proceeds with each side conceding a little ground until a compromise is reached somewhere between the two opening positions.

The result can fail all three criteria for a good negotiation. If one of the parties is much stronger than the other, their bargaining strength may have resulted in a contract that seriously undermines the financial stability of the other party. This is rarely an efficient process, as both parties may need to break off and consult other members of their organization before agreeing. Also, it is easy for one or the other of the parties to get locked into their bargaining position and for the whole process to become very confrontational. Concessions are then made in a spirit of bad will and the relationship can be severely and permanently damaged.

Successful long-term negotiations are what are commonly called win–win negotiations in which both sides come out of the negotiating process feeling that they have negotiated a good and fair result. There are several key steps to achieving a win–win result.

First, separate the people from the problem. Negotiations become confrontational when one party believes that they are personally being attacked or criticized. You must make sure that both parties recognize and understand what business issue is being negotiated. You should put yourself in the other people's shoes and understand their perception and needs. Communicate clearly and be an active listener. Don't fill the time while the other party is speaking by thinking of the next thing you want to say.

Second, you must invent options for mutual gain and use brain-storming techniques to evolve as many solutions as possible. Do not judge any idea prematurely, or search for a single answer, and don't ever think that solving their problem is their problem. You need to work together to solve problems.

Third, insist on objective criteria. The realities of life are such that even when trying for a win–win solution, there will inevitably be times when the interests of the two parties clash: you want delivery tomorrow, the supplier wants next week. When this happens you must insist on objective criteria for determining the outcome: for example, what is the industry standard?

SUMMARY

We have looked at one of the most crucial aspects of purchasing: determining the purchase price. The key considerations follow.

◆ There can be significant costs other than the initial purchase price involved in acquiring and using a purchased item; it is the total cost that buyers must reduce, not just the purchase price.

◆ There are potentially many factors that can persuade the selling company to modify its initial asking price; you need to understand what these factors are, and where and how to apply them.

◆ If you are to negotiate successfully, you need to analyze prices.

◆ If you want productive and effective long-term partnerships with suppliers, you must employ win–win approaches to negotiations. This means being hard but fair in your dealings with suppliers and searching for solutions that benefit both sides.

Chapter 6

Special Purchases

◆

Some categories of purchase are different from the ones you have described so far. These are:

◆ services.

◆ capital equipment.

◆ projects.

SERVICES

Every company needs a wide range of services to support its core activity. Examples are cleaning, advertising and promotions, maintenance of plant and equipment, and consultancy.

In many instances, the potential impact of these services can far outweigh the cost of the service bought. Consequently, the relationship between the specification of what is required, selecting the supplier, pricing the contract, and satisfying the end user, is complex. Getting the balance right is a key task for the buyer.

Specifying what is wanted

Previously we discussed the critical role that the specification plays in buying goods. This is equally true when buying services.

In many companies, the responsibility for developing the spec lies with the user. Good buyers can provide an invaluable service to the users by offering their knowledge and expertise in defining specs.

In some instances, it may even be beneficial to invite potential suppliers to assist in preparing the spec. This has two advantages. First, it enables you to use the contractor's expertise and knowledge and ensure that you are not over- or underspecifying critical aspects of the service. Second, it allows the potential contractors to get a better understanding of your organization and the level of effort that will be required to meet your expectations fully.

The first step in preparing the spec is to investigate the objectives of the contract and any constraints that have to be taken into account. The key tasks are:

◆ Deciding on the budget, timescales, and any other constraints that need to be taken into account.

◆ Defining the responsibilities of the different parties involved. For example, who will provide the materials to be used in the contract?

◆ Defining the tasks to be accomplished and the sequence of events needed to meet the overall contract deadlines. The buyer should challenge any key tasks and objectives already identified by the user, using value analysis techniques.

◆ Identifying any technical aspects, such as specifications.

The next step is to document your requirements. The same considerations you looked at in preparing specifications previously apply here. You must strike a balance between being clear as to what is needed and allowing the supplier sufficient scope to use individual initiative to meet the terms of the spec at the lowest cost.

Selecting the supplier

Selecting suppliers to fulfill service contracts can be more subjective than selecting suppliers of materials. The reason for this is that you are often buying a capability that is difficult to measure. For example, if you are running a chemical plant that operates 24 hours a day, you need a supplier of maintenance services to be able to respond quickly at any time of day or night, seven days a week, 52 weeks a year.

For this reason, a major factor when selecting suppliers of some key services may be the reputation of the supplier. This in itself may restrict your choice to a few suppliers, or even, in extreme cases, to just one.

The next step in the supplier selection process is to issue an invitation to bid to the shortlisted suppliers. When all the replies are received, the task of the buyer is to document the bids so they can be compared on the same basis.

Pricing the contract

If there are many potential suppliers of the service, competition may be sufficient to make sure that you pay a fair price. However, in some instances, there may be few potential suppliers or even just one. In other cases, it may not be clear at the outset just what extent of the service will be needed during the life of the contract. Under these circumstances, a mixture of good negotiation skills and an appropriate form of contract is needed.

The types of contracts available to you fall into three categories.

Fixed contracts are exactly what the name implies—the price is fixed at the start of the contract period. A firm fixed price contract is the most desirable because you will know exactly what you will be paying. However, some contracts extend over a long period and suppliers may be unwilling to face the risk of inflation in their costs. For these contracts, it may be fairer to build into the contract an agreed mechanism for increasing the contract price should the supplier's own costs increase by more than a certain amount.

Incentive contracts are more appropriate if there is a high degree of uncertainty about the effort needed to fulfill the contract or where the supplier can have an impact on costs through its own initiatives. Under these circumstances, a contract that acts as an incentive for the supplier to look at better and lower cost ways of performing the contract can be a benefit. An incentive contract usually has three components: a target price, a maximum price, and a formula for sharing any cost reductions below the target price.

Cost-based contracts differ from incentive contracts in that all the risk is borne by the customer. They should only be used when it is not possible to use either of the two previous contract types, because there is no incentive for the supplier to keep costs and, therefore, prices down. The supplier is reimbursed for any allowable costs and in addition is paid a fee for carrying out the service.

CAPITAL EQUIPMENT

Capital purchases are those items that are used on a continuing basis, unlike, say, raw materials that are consumed within a short space of time. They are items such as computers, machine tools, and forklift trucks.

It is important to get the purchase decision right the first time because the company will have to live with the consequences for many years. One strand of this decision-making process is to consider the life cycle costs of the purchase not just the initial purchase price. The cost of spare parts for maintaining and repairing a machine over its working life, for example, can be much greater than its purchase cost. Other costs include commissioning, training, and the eventual disposal of the machine.

Another aspect is the operating characteristics of the purchase. This is perhaps the most critical consideration when selecting the supplier, as seemingly identical items from different suppliers can behave quite differently in operation.

For all these reasons, capital buying is usually a team effort of the user, the buyer, and finance. In addition, the size of the buying may require the purchase to undergo a formal vetting and approval process by the company's senior management and board of directors.

PROJECTS
In many industries, new products require significant investment in design and development and can take many months to come to market. This is particularly true in high technology industries, such

as electronic equipment for defense applications, or in consumer markets where the unit price of the product is quite high (such as the automotive industry). The development of a new product is generally managed as a project.

It is not uncommon in these cases for 70 percent or more of the cost of the final product to be determined during the development phase. Buyers need to be involved at this early stage to make sure that purchases for the final design can be supplied at a cost that makes the new product competitive in the marketplace.

Buyers can have an impact in three main areas of a project's development.

◆ long-term supply market monitoring

◆ project cost control

◆ component cost control

Monitoring supply markets

The very nature of projects means that for key purchased items there are usually few capable suppliers, and the technology they use changes and evolves at a rapid rate. Just look at the specification of cars today compared even with five years ago. If you choose suppliers and technologies that are not up to date, you can suffer from a lack of competitiveness in your markets.

When monitoring supply markets, you should continually ask yourself these key questions:

◆ For the major components that you purchase, do you know where competing technologies are in their life cycle?

◆ Do you know what improvements in product performance your customers are demanding?

◆ Do you know what technical and commercial risks are associated with each technology?

◆ Do you know what new technological competencies you will need to develop with existing suppliers or source from new suppliers and when you will need them?

◆ Do you know what sort of relationship (partnership, alliance, codevelopment) you will need to develop with new suppliers?

◆ Do you know the volume of your future requirements and what this represents in terms of the size of the market?

◆ Do you know what barriers to entry or exit exist in the supply market?

◆ Do you know how costs behave in your supply markets?

The more *no* answers you get to these questions, the more you need to improve your systems for gathering and analyzing market intelligence. Buyers can play a key role in this technological scanning process by monitoring the performance of existing suppliers, and by searching for and developing new suppliers.

Project cost control

We saw earlier the way in which the specification of a purchase influences its cost. This is even more the case when buying for projects, as meeting the requirements of the user depends on sophisticated and expensive technology. You need to strike a balance between meeting the performance objectives of the product and controlling costs, so you can meet the pricing objectives of marketing and still make a profit.

The buyer needs to have special training and experience for projects. In addition to the expected buying skills, the buyer must be able to discuss the technological aspects of project buying with engineers and suppliers.

Many companies have achieved this by creating the role of purchasing engineer. This person is usually an engineer by training who has been assigned to the purchasing department for a period of time to learn the skills of buying. The tasks for the purchasing engineer follow.

1. Involve key suppliers before technological solutions are chosen for the project to make sure the choices are the best ones.

2. Assess the supply risks for the purchase elements of the project and produce a risk management plan.

3. Ensure that the overall project plan incorporates deadlines and workloads for the major purchasing tasks (for example, definition control, bidding process, design and change management).

4. Produce cost targets for the major purchased items based on the overall cost objectives for the project.

5. Initiate value analysis exercises for the major purchases.

6. Produce a control report that records planned and actual spending on purchases.

7. Monitor nonprice factors for purchases, such as quality and lead times.

8. Estimate the cost impact of design changes for purchased items.

Component cost control

In addition to managing the purchasing aspects of the total project, the purchasing engineer is also responsible for the purchase of the individual parts and subassemblies. The cost and delivery objectives of these are determined by the overall project plan. The buyer's task is to source them from the supply market in order to meet these objectives.

The process for buying the parts and subassemblies has a lot in common with the processes used for service and capital buying.

The starting point is to prepare a specification that meets the technological requirements of the overall project, but provides sufficient flexibility for the supplier to be innovative and cost competitive.

The technological scanning process described earlier will have identified the potential sources of supply. These will fall into one of two groups.

◆ partnership suppliers who have been involved in the design and specification of the purchased item

◆ a pool of suppliers who will be invited to bid on the purchase

The process is negotiating contracts with the first group on a win–win basis, or issuing invitations to bid to the second group. Both procedures were discussed earlier.

SUMMARY

There are some categories of purchase that need special treatment. These tend to be irregular or even one-time purchases such as services or capital equipment. In many cases you are buying a capability and not a product. It is critical that the specification of what you want to buy is clear and unambiguous.

Purchasing these items is usually done by a team rather than a single buyer. The buying role is to provide commercial expertise and supplier management skills to complement the technical specification skills of the other team members.

Chapter 7

Performance
Measures and
Continuous
Improvement

Performance measures can be powerful tools for motivating both buyers and suppliers to achieve your company aims and targets.

There is an old adage that says "what gets measured gets done." However, you must be very careful in setting performance measures, as they will determine the things that your buying department and suppliers see as priorities. This may work against what is best for the company overall.

For example, suppose you set a buyer a performance measure of processing 50 purchase orders a day. On one day, the buyer receives a purchase requisition for a product that is not a standard one. Should the buyer process the purchase order quickly in order to meet the target, or spend time on investigating potential sources, producing cost analyses, and finding out whether there is a cheaper way of meeting the user's requirements?

You need to keep several points in mind when deciding on the most appropriate performance measure for a particular buyer or supplier.

1. The activity must be simple to measure; if people do not understand how performance measures are calculated, they will not be motivated to improve.

2. The performance measure must be quantitative whenever possible. However, some activities will, by their very nature, be subjective. For example, if you select a supplier for design excellence, you will want to measure whether or not that supplier is contributing to your product design. This can only be measured subjectively by asking the design team for their views.

3. The person being measured must see a correlation between improvement in the activity and an improvement in the performance measure.

4. There must be quick feedback on the effect of changes in the activity. The longer the gap between performance and feedback, the less likely it is that the person concerned will be able to take corrective action.

5. The activity being measured must be under that person's direct control.

The key skill for the buyer is to select measures that will motivate both the external and internal teams to produce consistently world-class performance.

We saw previously that successful purchasing strategies are based on an understanding of the interrelationships between supply market complexity and the importance to you of the purchased item. You can use a similar approach to decide on the most appropriate performance measures, as shown in the diagram below.

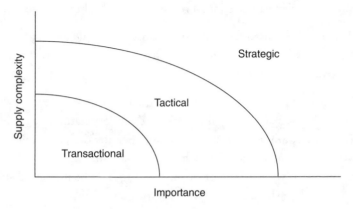

This diagram shows that there are three basic types of purchase, each requiring different performance measures.

Transactional buying

These are products that are predominantly in the noncritical quadrant of the purchase portfolio. You will remember that your strategy for these products was to procure them as efficiently as possible. Your performance measures, therefore, need to focus on efficiency.

Efficiency measures are ones that look at the outputs of a process and compare them to the inputs. The more output you get for a given input, the more efficient is the process.

$$\text{Efficiency} = \frac{\text{Output}}{\text{Input}}$$

Typical inputs to transactional buying are:

◆ cost (for example, overhead cost of the buying department).

◆ headcount.

◆ systems.

Typical outputs are:

◆ volume of transactions, such as purchase orders.

◆ error rates.

◆ number of suppliers.

Examples of performance measures that result from this are:

◆ number of suppliers per buyer.

◆ error rate per hundred purchase orders.

◆ number of purchase requisitions per $ invested in systems.

Applying this approach will give you a number of key ratios that measure the efficiency of your transaction buying processes. You can then monitor trends in the ratios and set targets for improvement. You can also compare the ratios for your business with those for others in the same industry using external surveys.

Tactical buying

The key measures for this group should reflect the effectiveness of the buying process. There are many measures that can be used, and it is up to the buyer to decide which are the most appropriate for the specific needs of the company.

The timing of deliveries is a key measure for most companies. The buyer's first responsibility is to support the company's line operations and ensure that supplies are available when needed. You can measure your effectiveness in doing this by monitoring

◆ the percentage of overdue orders.

◆ the percentage of stockouts caused by late deliveries.

◆ number or production stoppages caused by later deliveries.

◆ actual delivery date compared with supplier's promised delivery date.

Deliveries may be on time but still cause problems because incorrect quantities were delivered. Therefore, you need some measure of the effectiveness of the process for getting the correct quantity. Typical measures are:

◆ actual service level achieved by stock levels compared with target.

◆ delivery quantity compared to order quantity.

◆ stock turnover.

◆ report on stock surpluses due to overbuying.

◆ value of supplier stockholdings negotiated by the buyer.

◆ percentage of orders for which incorrect items were sent.

◆ percentage of orders for which split shipments were sent.

◆ quality of transportation used as measured by damaged shipments and incorrect documentation.

A useful way to show measures such as delivery performance is with a graph.

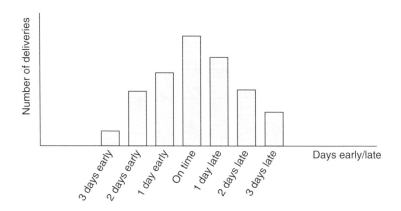

One chemical company uses this approach and measures each delivery from a supplier to see if it was on time in full. The answer is either yes or no. If the supplier gets five no's out of 100 deliveries it is put on the "sick list." If it drops to 10 out of 100, that supplier is no longer used.

Another key measure of effectiveness is the quality of the items purchased. Some useful measures for this are:

◆ percentage of items rejected.

◆ percentage of batches rejected.

◆ number of suppliers that have been certified by your quality team.

◆ number of suppliers using statistical process control techniques.

Strategic purchases

You need to change the emphasis in performance measures to reflect the requirements of strategic purchases. The measures used for tactical buying change can be illustrated like this.

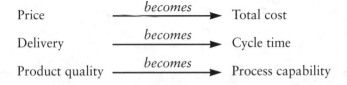

Total cost means all the costs associated with a purchase and not just the initial purchase price. This means, for example, the cost of holding stock to allow for long lead times, the cost of rework if the item fails in your production process, and the cost of warranties if your product fails when used by a customer and the failure is attributable to the purchased part.

These costs are often hidden by accounting systems in the sense that they are not analyzed and identified with a purchase, but are charged to accounts such as repair or warranty. You may find that changes are needed in your systems to allow you to calculate a true cost for a purchase.

Cycle time measures are aimed at the processes that affect your ability to meet customer demand as quickly as possible. They cover areas such as the time to develop a new prototype, manufacturing process times, order processing times, and delivery transit times.

The shorter your supplier can makes these times, the more flexible and responsive you can become.

For transactional and tactical buying the most practical way of measuring quality is to choose suppliers who adhere to a specific standard or have achieved some external certification such as ISO 9000. You need to be more rigorous for strategic buying and take all precautions to make sure that you receive a quality product.

You can achieve this by assessing the supplier's production process and satisfying yourselves that it is capable of manufacturing to the tolerances you require. Ongoing performance measures are then aimed at monitoring the process to make sure that it is performing to that quality. One way to do this is through statistical process control.

Performance measures for the buying department then revolve around the number of suppliers who have implemented statistical process control techniques and their continued adherence to them.

SETTING TARGETS

It is not enough to measure current performance. You need to set improvement targets for yourselves and your suppliers. How do you do this so that the targets are challenging but still fair?

Brian Maskell, in his book *Performance Measurement for World-Class Manufacturing*, discusses the concept of half lives. A study of a large number of companies undergoing improvement projects showed that the rates of improvement exhibited similar patterns even though the problems being addressed were different.

The conclusion drawn is that rates of improvement are consistent and can be expressed in terms of the time taken to halve the problem. For example, if it takes three months to halve the error rate in processing purchase orders from 4 percent to 2 percent, it will take another three months to halve the rate again to 1 percent.

The rule of thumb to use in setting targets is that for a situation under the direct control of one department or one supplier, the half life is typically three months. If you need cooperation to tackle the problem, the half life is typically nine months.

COMPETITIVE BENCHMARKING

What is now generally called competitive benchmarking started at Xerox Corporation in 1979. Faced with mounting competition for its photocopier products, Xerox set about systematically comparing its operations with competitors with the aim of finding out what competitors did differently and better.

Robert C. Camp has documented the results of this process in his book *Benchmarking: The Search for Industry Best Practices that Lead to Superior Performance*.

The purpose of benchmarking is to find the most effective way to meet customer requirements and obtain customer satisfaction. Purchasing is one very important function in any company that contributes to these goals. Applying benchmarking concepts to purchasing can provide valuable insights into how to improve. It is a powerful tool for setting performance measures.

Camp identifies a 10-step process for carrying out a successful benchmarking exercise. You have to:

1. Identify what is to be benchmarked. Purchasing, like any other business function, is comprised of different processes, each of which has an output. An example of this is the process for administering purchase orders that has a valid purchase order as its output. The key processes that contribute to the company's mission of satisfying customers need to be identified.

2. Decide on the company or companies with whom you want to compare your processes. You need to consider not only the leaders in your industry, but also leading companies in other

industries. After all, the aim is to outperform the best in your industry, not just achieve the same level as the best.

3. Decide how you will collect the data. This is not only hard data that measure the process being benchmarked, but also data on how best practice methods are performed.

4. Determine the current gap between your process performance and that of the best practice leader. The gap will indicate the effort needed to close the gap.

5. Project future performance levels. Unless you take action, is the gap going to get bigger? What are the consequences of this for your company?

6. Communicate benchmark findings and get acceptance. Unless you demonstrate convincing findings based on hard data, you will not get the resources and support you need to make change happen.

7. Establish goals. As with all performance measures and targets, these need to be challenging but at the same time credible if they are to be motivating.

8. Develop action plans. The people who actually carry out the work tasks are usually in the best position to determine how the benchmark findings can be incorporated into current work practices. Make sure you involve these people.

9. Implement actions and measure progress.

10. Recalibrate benchmarks. Business life is not static. Competitors and best practice leaders in other industries will also be taking steps to improve. You need to revisit benchmarks from time to

time to make sure that the targets and plans you have put in place are still relevant.

A company is not long for this world if it doesn't know how to control its buying costs. Here are some basic tips that may help you to control your costs by being intelligent about how you buy.

1. **Limit who can order.** Many successful companies today centralize their purchasing operation so that one person or one department is totally responsible for all the purchasing. In this way, every order request is channeled to a specific area. This gives the company far better control and thereby reduces the chance of order duplications and minimizes purchasing errors.

2. **Buy in bulk.** It is usually more economical to order in bulk when the price per unit is often less than it would be on an individual basis. Bulk ordering also cuts down on the time your personnel spend constantly cranking reorders into the system. However, before you go ahead and order in bulk, consider whether (a) you have room for this merchandise, and (b) if you expect to be able to sell or use it quickly.

   Bulk buying enables you to set favorable prices because of the large order coupled with a long-term commitment. A form of bulk buying is standardized buying where you agree to purchase the same product over and over. As a result, you generally receive the same lower per-unit price, no matter how many units you order.

3. **Maximize discounts.** Most suppliers offer discounts not only for ordering large quantities of a product but also by making payments within a specific period of time. In this way, you receive the advantage of having a certain percentage deducted from the purchase price if you pay your bill within so many days or even months. The numbers vary, but you generally can negotiate fairly

good terms based on what the traffic in the particular industry will bear.

4. **Use suppliers' expertise.** Your suppliers are usually willing to help you find ways to reduce your costs. But you must let your suppliers know what your problems are so they can work with you in minimizing such expenditures. This covers a wide range of areas including pricing, delivery, and payments. The suppliers' input can show you how you can make purchases more intelligently and thereby reduce ordering and billing costs.

A technique used by many suppliers that has proven most successful is the automatic ordering system. This enables the supplier to come to your company and check your stock on a regular basis (usually monthly). The supplier can then replenish those items that are in short supply—immediately and at a prefixed price. The beauty of this arrangement is that it keeps your stock fresh and plentiful at all times. The last thing you want to do is run out of what you need.

5. **Negotiate, negotiate, negotiate.** Nothing is set in stone. It makes sense to send items out for bid so you can get the best prices and terms available. There is always another supplier out there who will want to do the job and will furnish the materials faster and at a lower cost. However, keep in mind that cheap doesn't necessarily mean good.

6. **Put it in writing.** Paperwork in the form of proposals, competitive bidding sheets, sales agreements, purchase orders, invoices, delivery documents, and the like must be prepared when dealing with any supplier. If a dispute arises, having this paperwork will save you aggravation and money.

SUMMARY

This chapter examined ways of assisting your efforts to become the best in your industry in the key purchasing processes, specifically:

◆ performance measures for transactional, tactical, and strategic purchasing.

◆ how to set targets that are challenging but at the same time motivating.

◆ benchmarking as a way to become the industry leader—and just as important, to stay the leader.

INDEX